GOD'S GIFT FOR A GOOD NIGHT'S SLEEP

STACEY SPELLER

Printed in the United States of America

First Printing, 2017

ISBN 978-0-9798916-3-2

Speak2Stacey LLC
10 Glen Lake Parkway, Suite 130
Atlanta, GA 30328

www.staceyspeller.com

To Bradie who always loves,
supports and believes.
You are the husband I prayed for
and I love you to life.

Intro

One of the greatest challenges I had to overcome was the ability to get a good night's sleep. I was that girl who either fell into bed exhausted after an 18-hour day only to sleep for a few hours, or I would consciously plan to get the appropriate seven to eight hours of sleep, but would inevitably end up tossing and turning throughout the night, again, getting little sleep. I couldn't turn off my brain! The quiet darkness of my bedroom seemed to provide the fuel for my thoughts to spiral out of control. It also didn't help that I kept a notepad and pen on my nightstand just in case I thought of something I needed to do, so these instruments called to me through the night saying write this down!

Intellectually, I knew the importance of getting the proper sleep, both quantity and quality. After all, I had spent enough of those sleepless nights googling the effects of poor sleep habits: low performance, health challenges, poor decision-making, aging skin and even weight gain being some of the downsides to poor sleep habits. YIKES! Making bad decisions! Looking old, being out of shape and overweight! These reason alone should be motivation enough for any woman to make some changes, but sadly for me . . . it was not enough.

I rationalized about my lack of sleep by adopting what I thought to be the mindset of the perfect person; meaning, when my life became less stressful, more peaceful and I didn't have too much on my plate, then I could sleep. Right now, however, sleep was an overpriced luxury I just could not afford in my quest to hold it all together, to make ends meet and make sense of everything life threw my way. So I continued justifying my lack of sleep the same way you may be doing right now in your situation: you're a single-mom, a working professional with a demanding career, a single woman with far too much on her plate, a middle-aged woman caring not only your family but also for your elderly parents. These are very real and legitimate scenarios for women in today's world. Who can sleep when there is so much to do?

Regardless of how much I tried to justify my lack of sleep, there really wasn't a good reason for it. God speaks of sleep being a gift He gives to us, and that it should restore us and be sweet. Well, my sleep was anything but restorative and sweet. In August of 2012, a day I remember like yesterday, I finally woke up to my truth. Midway through a night of tossing and turning with my brain going 100 miles per hour, I looked over at my husband Bradie who was sleeping soundly. I could have driven a truck in our bedroom and he wouldn't have budged!

In complete annoyance at his contented sleep, I did the unthinkable. I elbowed him quite hard and told him to GET UP and worry with me! How dare he sleep peacefully knowing that we had so many challenges going on in life? There were decisions to be made and things to get done! In all transparency, I was actually resentful that my husband was doing what God said, to sleep and refresh. Bradie gave me a side-eye and told me that if I wanted to stay up, good for me, he however, was going back to sleep! I tip-toed out of the bedroom and went to decide what I wanted to work on during the wee hours of the night, leaving Bradie again sleeping soundly.

As I sat on the couch trying to decide between returning emails or organizing my pantry, the Holy Spirit directed me to Psalm 127:2, *"It's useless to rise early and go to bed late, and work your worried fingers to the bone. Don't you know He enjoys giving rest to those He loves?"* (The Message).

WOW! "My worried fingers" that was my problem! In that moment, I realized my biggest barrier to sleep was my lack of trust in God. I was anxious, worried, and fearful, all the things The Bible speaks against, and I was doing all of these things in major doses. No matter how much I attended church and served in different ministries, my uncomfortable truth was that I didn't know how to truly cast my cares, and to leave them at His feet. The night I elbowed my husband was the night I made a big decision: to become fully aware that there is only ONE God and I am not Him.

I CAN turn it off, CAN shut down and sleep and the world still goes on. The moon will stay in the sky and the sun will still rise even if I'm off duty for a while getting some much-needed sleep. I don't need to be ALL things to ALL people, I don't need to solve every problem and I don't need to fight every battle. Being still and knowing that He is God became my nightly mediation.

It has been five years now, and while I don't get perfect sleep every night, I have become intentional. Regardless of what is going on, I am intentional about prioritizing my life for maximum productivity by day, which means I am intentional about getting proper sleep and I therefore, turn it all over to God every night.

Fast forward to a few years later when a friend was complaining about a particular situation that was keeping her awake at night. She asked my advice via text message and the next day she reached out and told me that what I texted back was powerful and had helped her enormously. She then suggested that I share the message with others.

I took up her suggestion and posted my exact message to her on my social media pages knowing that only God knew how much the message could be used to help or bless others, or even to spark a movement of sorts. Right after the posting, I started to receive e-mails and comments. Then conversations started happening around the concept of ways to *Rest Well*, and the idea took off!

Rest Well has afforded me the opportunity to speak with so many women who struggle with being able to sleep. Thousands of women from all different walks of life have crossed my path either in person or online; from a CEO in Europe, to a stay-at-home mom in Kansas, even a biological engineer in Los Angeles! It didn't matter what education level, profession, or culture, women everywhere could relate to not sleeping, and were looking for answers.

Therefore, I purposed myself to share what was in my heart, to help women overcome the things that keep them awake at night. I am a firm believer that God blesses us to overcome our challenges so we can then help others do the same. This Devotional is written from the heart, from real life experiences and from the amazing lessons God has taught me.

I encourage you to stick with the process, invest the time nightly and stay the course. I promise that if you commit the next 90 days the journey, the priceless gifts of peace, joy, purpose and clarity will become your new normal when you truly learn how to rest in God and *Rest Well.*

WELCOME TO THE FIRST Ninety DAYS OF THE REST OF YOUR LIFE!

Stacey

Stacey Speller
Success Coach, CEO Speak2Stacey
Creator of Life Mastery School for Ambitious Women

New You

REST WELL KNOWING THAT EVERYTHING THAT'S HAPPENED IN THE PAST HAS PREPARED YOU FOR BLESSINGS NOW AND IN YOUR FUTURE.

Sometimes the hardest part about moving forward comes from trying to find balance as you straddle the fence; in one hand holding onto every negative thing that happened previously, and in the other hand, holding onto the excitement and possibilities of a new beginning. The hurt, the upset, the offense, and the disappointment of the past are all very real and present to you. Even though you recognize that it is a season of new beginnings, you are still bothered by the issues from last season. But now you know better and realize that past issues are a distant memory compared to present blessings. You are too busy speaking life into your promise to continue tripping over the same old problems. You know that God told you to cast your cares upon Him and leave them there. So Rest Well knowing that you can let go of any bad experience from the past and embrace every lesson you learned because by doing so, you are so well-prepared for the blessings of your new beginnings.

"And the one sitting on the throne said, 'Look, I am making everything new!' And then He said to me, 'Write this down, for what I tell you is trustworthy and true'" (Revelation 21:5, NLT).

Dear God

I thank You for new beginnings and I embrace the newness of this season with praise and thanksgiving.

Notes

REST WELL KNOWING THAT TODAY WAS THE LAST DAY YOU TOLERATED ANYTHING LESS THAN GOD'S BEST FOR YOUR LIFE.

Sometimes you can find yourself lowering your standards and downgrading your dreams to accommodate your circumstance or your environment. You see that everyone around you is struggling, settling for less and trying to survive from day to day. Your emotions take notice of all the negativity around you and you start to question, is this as good as it gets? But now you know better and realize that in this new season, living in your promise and experiencing God's best is a decision you are fully-prepared to make because anything less is unacceptable. You know that even though you are only a few days into your new season, today was the last day that mediocrity made itself at home in your life. So Rest Well knowing that you have a made-up mind for God's best and you are not backing down, but looking up with great anticipation.

"Since this new way gives us confidence, we can be very bold" (2 Corinthians3:12, NLT).

Dear God

I trust that Your word is true and I am going to boldly expect Your best with a made-up mind and Godly patience.

Notes

REST WELL KNOWING THAT THE UNCERTAINTY OF A NEW SEASON IS NOT YOUR PORTION BECAUSE GOD IS THE SAME YESTERDAY, TODAY AND FOREVER.

Sometimes new beginnings bring on unnecessary stress and confusion. You know it is a time for change and for things to be different, but these changes may cause you to overthink the wrong things. Wondering what comes next and being overly-concerned about what the future holds is stressful. At times, the world seems to be upside-down with everything from crazy temperatures to world terrorism, and if you're honest, new and different can be scary. But now you know better and realize that God did not give you a spirit full of fear, but a spirit full of peace and power. That what causes angst and stress for others causes you to thank God for His grace and protection. You know that His good report did not change just because you turned the page on your calendar. So Rest Well knowing that worry is not your portion and there is no uncertainty in the Kingdom because God's faithfulness is the same.

"Jesus Christ is the same yesterday, today, and forever" (Hebrews13:8, NLT).

Dear God

I thank You that in spite of any uncertainty in my life, You give me continuity and stability in every season.

Notes

REST WELL KNOWING THAT YOU DON'T NEED A RESOLUTION TO IMPROVE YOUR LIFE BECAUSE YOUR RENEWED MIND IS YOUR GAME-CHANGER.

Sometimes you get so bombarded with the concept of making resolutions. Every New Year millions of people go through this useless exercise of claiming to make this year the best yet by implementing lasting change. At the end of every year those same people are wondering why they did not accomplish much of anything and instead experienced more of the same. But now you know better and realize that more of the same is not your portion, you are wiser than ever and you know that renewing your mind trumps a resolution any day. You know that the keys to the Kingdom don't come by resolution, they happen with revelation, and a renewed mind does not need to resolve anything, it is already full of everything. So Rest Well knowing that you won't experience the regret of a failed resolution because your renewed mind is your game-changer.

"Don't copy the behavior and customs of this world, but let God transform you into a new person by changing the way you think. Then you will learn to know God's will for you, which is good and pleasing and perfect" (Romans12:2, NLT).

Dear God

This year I will achieve my goals because my mind is renewed to Your perfect will.

Notes

REST WELL KNOWING THAT YOUR PROGRESS IS NOT MEASURED BY TIME, IT IS MEASURED BY POSSIBILITIES.

Sometimes you discount your accomplishments and miscount your blessings because you're racing against an imaginary clock. It is a new season and your feelings make you anxious about your station in life. You consider how long you've been pressing, how much time you've spent trying to achieve your goals, and how long you've been standing on your promise or trying to bring the walls down. You've manufactured unnecessary stress in your life because you're trying to compare your progress with someone else's finished product. But now you know better and realize that the best things come to those who don't waiver and refuse to give up. And you know that the walls don't come down the first time around but persistence leads to your promise. So Rest Well knowing that your progress has absolutely nothing to do with how long it has been and everything to do with the fact that with God, all things become possible.

"So let's not get tired of doing what is good. At just the right time we will reap a harvest of blessing if we don't give up" (Galatians 6:9, NLT).

Dear God

I thank You for divine possibilities and I'm not giving up because I trust You for my harvest of blessings.

Notes

REST WELL KNOWING THAT YOU ARE WALKING BY FAITH AND TURNING BACK IS NOT AN OPTION.

Sometimes you find yourself walking by sight and you do not like what you see. What's in front of you is unfamiliar and it's causing you to have doubts. The unknown is overwhelming, it is intimidating and now you're really starting to question your faith decision. Truth be told, it is tempting to revert back to past habits and expectations. You are more comfortable when things are familiar even if it causes you to live beneath your promise. But now you know better and realize that you walk by faith, not by sight. You are not going to stay bound to your familiar place, you are going forward into your blessed place. What you thought was overwhelming is really exceeding and abundant. So Rest Well knowing that you have come too far and God is too faithful for you to turn back now.

"The Lord says, 'I will guide you along the best pathway for your life. I will advise you and watch over you'" (Psalm 32:8, NLT).

Dear God

I am grateful for Your guidance and watchful faithfulness. I trust that You know the best direction for my life.

Notes

REST WELL KNOWING THAT GOD'S GOT YOUR BACK AND YOU HAVE NOTHING TO FEAR BY MOVING FORWARD.

Sometimes you find yourself confused by the fact that the people you have blessed are not always willing and available to reciprocate that blessing. It seems logical that since you helped them, they would be the ones to have your back and look out for you. Now you feel like you are out on a limb because you stepped out on faith thinking certain people would be there for you, and yet they are nowhere to be found. But now you know better and realize God has already assigned people who are going to favor you with blessings, regardless of who is not helping you. Remind yourself that God is for you in spite of who is not available to you. So Rest Well knowing that God's got your back and you can move forward with confidence.

"But Moses told the people, 'Don't be afraid. Just stand still and watch the LORD rescue you today. The Egyptians you see today will never be seen again'" (Exodus14:13, NLT).

Dear God

I thank You that even when it feels like I'm out on a limb, You are my safety net that will always rescue me in my time of trouble.

Notes

Moving
Forward

REST WELL KNOWING THAT THERE IS NO SHAME IN SECOND CHANCES.

Sometimes guilt and regret will cause you to forget that the God you serve specializes in second chances. You spend so much time thinking about what happened, what didn't work out, and where you may have gone wrong that you end up staying stuck in the past. Then the busy-bodies who profess to love God tell you to just give up and throw in the towel. But now you know better and realize that is not what the word says. God said He has nothing but love for you and that He is patient with you. He cares for you, He helps you and He keeps you from being disgraced. So Rest Well knowing that you are about to experience heaven's exchange program where God gives you a double-portion of love and forgiveness for any shame you have encountered and you will soon be rejoicing over what you thought was your disgrace.

"To all who mourn in Israel, He will give a crown of beauty for ashes, a joyous blessing instead of mourning, festive praise instead of despair" (Isaiah 61:3, NLT).

Dear God

I gladly surrender my ashes for Your crown of beauty and seize my second chance to experience Your best.

Notes

REST WELL KNOWING THAT YOUR LATTER SHALL BE GREATER BECAUSE NOW YOU KNOW BETTER.

Sometimes it's easy to despise your mistakes because they have wreaked so much havoc in your life. You don't know what you were thinking and you cannot believe you allowed yourself to go so far off the beaten path. Your negative feelings are completely committed to your mess-up, they won't let you forget about it and move on. The voice of doubt hijacks your peace and causes you to walk in un-forgiveness toward your former self. You have condemned and punished yourself by limiting your thinking to the level of your mistake. But now you know better and realize that God has already forgiven you. You know that He has not changed His mind concerning you, and that you are not disqualified from experiencing the desires of your heart. So Rest Well knowing that you are wiser than ever before and your latter is going to be so much more blessed because now you know The Truth.

"The godly may trip seven times, but they will get up again. But one disaster is enough to overthrow the wicked" (Proverbs24:16, NLT).

Dear God

I speak life over my latter days knowing that I have Your righteousness and godliness and will recover from anything in my past.

Notes

REST WELL KNOWING THAT YOU HAVE BEEN GIVEN A NEW LEASE ON LIFE AND YOU CAN STOP PAYING RENT TO YOUR OLD SITUATIONS.

Sometimes what distracts you from your second-chance opportunity comes from your first-time mistake. Somehow you have believed the hype that you owe your past some debt that can never be paid and you feel obligated to stay connected to the negativity of your past. The voice of doubt does not want you to move forward, so you stay stuck somewhere between your former self and your best self. But now you know better and realize that the greatest debt was paid on Calvary. You know that you serve a mighty God who specializes in giving you a fresh start, a new beginning, a do-over. He wipes the slate clean by throwing all of your mess into His Sea of Forgetfulness. So Rest Well knowing that the old has passed away, you have a divine opportunity in front of you and it is okay to close the door on what is behind you.

"No dear brothers and sisters, I have not achieved it, but I focus on this one thing: Forgetting the past and looking forward to what lies ahead" (Philippians3:13, NLT).

Dear God

I release any old situation and move forward from any closed door knowing that I can trust You with what lies ahead of me.

Notes

REST WELL KNOWING THAT WHEN GOD SAYS DO NOT LOOK BACK, IT IS BECAUSE BETTER IS UP AHEAD.

Sometimes you are walking by faith surrounded by serious doubts about what comes next. God's word said to move forward but you are hard-pressed to let go of what is behind you. What is behind you is comfortable, it's familiar and you either don't want to give it up, or you don't know how. Truth be told, your feelings start negotiating with your faith, trying to reach a settlement agreement, trying to find a way to visit your past and stay in touch, even though it means you no good. But now you know better and realize that compromise is the language of fear, and you speak fluent faith. You are not backing down because standing strong is how you inherit your promise. You know that comfortable is a distraction to keep you from God's best. So Rest Well knowing that when God says to move forward, don't look back because BETTER is up ahead.

"If they had been thinking of the country they had left, they would have had opportunity to return" (Hebrews11:15, NIV).

Dear God

I am going to release my thoughts from what I left and embrace where I am going by Your grace.

Notes

REST WELL KNOWING THAT GOD'S ABILITY TO TURN THINGS AROUND IS NOT LIMITED BY ANYONE WHO IS TRYING TO HOLD YOU BACK.

Sometimes your negative thoughts will empower someone who is interfering with your forward progress. You spend far too much time trying to understand why they are so determined to be a thorn in your side, why they don't support your growth, and why they want to invest in your failure. Your emotions get involved and overdramatize someone else's ability to impact your destiny, to derail your dreams or somehow keep you from your promised place. But now you know better and you remember that no weapon formed against you can prosper. You know that if God can be for you, who can be against you? And you know that God specializes in comebacks and turnarounds. So Rest Well knowing that the God of ALL things possible is not in the least bit limited or intimidated by anyone trying to come against the desires of your heart.

"Then the Lord said to Moses, 'Why are you crying out to me? Tell the people to get moving!'" (Exodus14:15, NLT).

Dear God

I am confident that You will turn my situation around in spite of anything trying to hold me back. I will move on.

Notes

REST WELL KNOWING THAT YOU MAY NOT BE WHERE YOU WANT TO BE, BUT PRAISE GOD THAT YOU ARE NO LONGER WHERE YOU USED TO BE.

Sometimes you get overwhelmed by how much further it seems you have to go before you witness your breakthrough, reach your goals, and occupy your promise. You have been pressing and marching, but it feels like whenever you take a step forward, there are still many more steps to climb. The voice of doubt tells you to dial it down because you shouldn't have stepped out of the boat considering you are the least-likely to succeed. But now you know better and realize the enemy cannot measure your progress for something that God has already promised. You know that the walls may not come down the first time around, but consistency will cause them to fall, and you have come too far to let a lie turn you back. So Rest Well knowing that you may not be where you want to be yet, but praise God you're on your way.

"I'm off and running, and I'm not turning back" (Philippians 3:14, The Message).

Dear God

I thank You and I celebrate the progress I have made knowing that You have equipped me to keep going forward by faith.

Notes

REST WELL KNOWING THAT MERCY HAS ALREADY REWRITTEN YOUR PAST SO YOU CAN CREATE A BETTER FUTURE.

Sometimes what keeps you from embracing better comes from holding on to your past. You cannot seem to let go of who you used to be, what you've done, or where you've been. Even the company you keep finds a way to keep you mindful of your former identity and they make it really hard for you to see yourself as a new creation. Eventually you create a self-imposed anchor to the missteps you made in life. The voice of doubt tries to convince you that a blessed life is for people who didn't have a messed-up past. But now you know better and realize that God is so faithful that His mercy has already reconciled your past. You know that He has a plan for you that trumps anything you've been through. So Rest Well knowing that your latter will be greater because God's mercy has already rewritten your story.

"God rewrote the text of my life when I opened the book of my heart to His eyes" (2 Samuel 22:25, The Message).

Dear God

I thank You that my eyes are opened to the knowledge that Your mercy has already rewritten my story and the end of the book says I win.

Notes

Hope

REST WELL KNOWING THAT WHEN GOD ASKS YOU, "WHAT IS THAT IN YOUR HAND?" IT IS BECAUSE YOUR BREAKTHROUGH IS WITHIN REACH.

Sometimes you can waste so much time worrying that you aren't enough and you're ill-equipped for the task at hand. You have no clue what comes next and you're anxious trying to figure out how God is going to bring you out. It is really hard to trust God because you're leaning on your own understanding and it doesn't make sense. But now you know better and realize that God said, "Now faith is" because He is a present help for exactly what you're experiencing. He knows the end from the beginning with a plan to bring you out even before you went in, and He has a proven track record for using the ordinary to accomplish the extra-ordinary. So Rest Well knowing that when God asks what is in your hand, He doesn't need you to answer, He wants you to know and trust that your breakthrough is at hand.

"Then the Lord said to him, 'What is that in your hand?' 'A staff,' he replied" (Exodus 4:2, NIV).

Dear God

I submit what I have to You knowing that in Your hands a simple stick can become a powerful tool to bring me out.

Notes

REST WELL KNOWING THAT DIFFICULT TIMES ALWAYS GIVE WAY TO "BUT GOD" MOMENTS.

Sometimes you are walking by faith and you hit a rough patch in the road, an obstacle, perhaps even a mountain. You are very confused by what is happening since it seemed like you were doing your best to get everything right. You start searching your history looking for clues that would help you understand why it looks like God has abandoned you, or worse, He is punishing you. But now you know better and realize that obstacles are just opportunities for God to show Himself able. You know that you don't need to try and get it right, God has already declared you righteous, and you have hope for the future knowing you are already forgiven. So Rest Well knowing that a difficult time is temporary but it always gives way to those "But God" moments when you will look back and know that you know it was nothing but the Lord on your side.

"I say to myself, 'The Lord is my inheritance; therefore, I will hope in Him!'" (Lamentations 3:24, NLT).

Dear God

In the midst of any difficulty I put my hope in You knowing that my situation is temporary but Your love for me is everlasting.

Notes

REST WELL KNOWING THAT THE FIRST REPORT IS NOT THE FINAL WORD.

Whenever you are hit with what looks like bad news, your negative emotions are on the ready to bring you into a place of fear, unbelief, stress and worry. Things look bad, and there doesn't seem to be any possible way to keep hope alive. Eventually you become so full of despair that doubt becomes your new normal. But just when you are about to give the benediction over your circumstance, you remember the message of the cross: everyone thought the crucifixion was the end, their faith was in vain and somehow they missed God. But now you know better and realize that even though the cross looked like all hope was gone, it became the greatest source of hope, and your faith is strong for such a time as this. So Rest Well knowing that the first report is never the last report and God ALWAYS gets the last word.

"For nothing will be impossible with God" (Luke 1:37, ESV).

Dear God

I thank You for the right report that reminds me what I think is a giant in my life is really just a grasshopper that will not stand in my way.

Notes

REST WELL KNOWING THAT WHEN YOU SEEK FIRST GOD'S KINGDOM, YOU WILL ALWAYS FIND EVERYTHING YOU NEED.

Sometimes you find yourself lacking because you are looking for solutions in all the wrong places. Frustration sets in because it seems like no matter what you try, it doesn't seem to work out. You take advice from your past experiences as if what you have been through is any indication of what God has prepared for you. Your feelings start to spiral out of control. But now you know better and recognize that God already promised when you make Him and His plans your priority, He will add everything you need into your life. You know that your faith fuels your hope because you know that God does not disappoint as He is a rewarder. So Rest Well knowing that you do not need to waste time trying to find answers in all the wrong places, just spend time seeking His face and you will find everything you need.

"Seek the Kingdom of God above all else, and live righteously, and He will give you everything you need" (Matthew 6:33, NLT).

Dear God

I release all of my frustration and look to You for my solutions knowing You have already provided everything I need.

Notes

REST WELL KNOWING THAT GOD ALWAYS HAS MORE THAN ONE WAY TO GIVE YOU THE DESIRES OF YOUR HEART.

Sometimes when things don't work out the way you thought, you get distracted by disappointment. It's like you cannot get past what didn't work out and you start wondering if things will ever turn in your favor. You were so confident in how you expected God to bless you and when it doesn't come to pass, you start doubting if He ever will bless you. But now you know better and realize that God's thoughts are higher than your thoughts, and you know that He is too strategic to be limited by how you thought He should bless you. It is His good pleasure for you to experience life exceedingly and abundantly and whatever didn't work out, God is still going to have His way. So Rest Well knowing God has more than one way to give you the desires of your heart and what He has planned is well beyond what you could ask or think.

"You will be rewarded for this; your hope will not be disappointed" (Proverbs 23:18, NLT).

Dear God

I know You are able to bless me beyond what I could ask or think and I have renewed hope because I know that You are more than able.

Notes

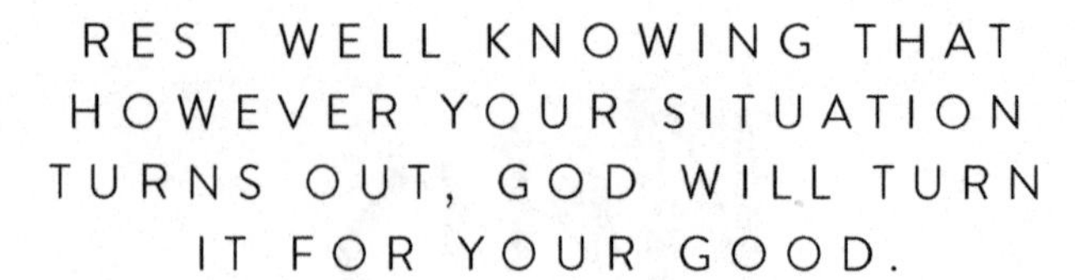

REST WELL KNOWING THAT HOWEVER YOUR SITUATION TURNS OUT, GOD WILL TURN IT FOR YOUR GOOD.

Sometimes in the midst of a difficult situation you cannot imagine how anything good can come out of it. You tell yourself to just endure and look forward to a "microwaved" ending to the entire ordeal. Negative feelings will tell you that this must be the worst thing ever and the voice of doubt provides immediate confirmation. You lower your expectations to the point of trying to merely survive the situation and hope that one day you can just put it all behind you. But now you know better and realize you are not just a survivor, you are an overcomer. You know that your expectations do not come from what you're experiencing, they come from what you've been promised. So Rest Well knowing that the same God who can take you from the pit to the palace will use even the worst situations to become a set-up for your greatest blessings.

"May the God of hope fill you with all joy and peace in believing, so that by the power of the Holy Spirit you may abound in hope" (Romans 15:13, NIV).

Dear God

I graciously receive the hope which You have given me and I know You will cause me to overcome anything I am experiencing.

Notes

REST WELL KNOWING THAT WHEN GOD WORKS IT'S FOR GOOD, YOUR STUMBLING BLOCK WILL BECOME YOUR STEPPING STONE.

Sometimes you trip over the wrong things, you stumble into fruitless situations, and you find yourself repeatedly getting knocked down. Your intentions are good, but you find yourself acting on what you see instead of what you believe. The more you try to press through, to keep moving forward over that same mountain, the more trips you continue to make. Hope is starting to seem more like a pipe dream than a reality. But now you know better and realize that God is still able to make your crooked paths straight. You know that your steps are ordered, and God has already provided His grace to help you get back up again and run your race. God uses ALL things for His good purpose. So Rest Well knowing that what once was a stumbling block is being transformed into your stepping stone to ALL of God's best.

"Then you will walk in your way securely and your foot will not stumble" (Proverbs 3:23, ESV).

Dear God

I will stop tripping over my obstacles and start trusting You to use them as my stepping stones into greatness.

Notes

REST WELL KNOWING THAT YOUR NEXT LEVEL IS ABOUT "WHO" YOU'RE CONNECTED TO, NOT LIMITED BY WHO YOU KNOW.

Sometimes you are striving with all of your might to go to your next level. You want to advance in your career, your finances, or your relationship. The challenge is that you've accepted input from your unbelief and you are focused on what you don't have: not enough education, not the right contacts, nor the relevant experience. To make matters worse, the company you keep has become the Amen chorus for the voice of doubt. But now you know better and realize that it doesn't matter who you know because your promotion comes from the Lord, an open mind and a hopeful heart will bring about divine connections and His favor gives you unimaginable advantages. So Rest Well knowing that your next level of abundance won't be limited by who you know because you are connected to the True Vine and He will cause you to bear much fruit.

"God can pour on the blessings in astonishing ways so that you're ready for anything and everything, more than just ready to do what needs to be done" (2 Corinthians 9:8, The Message).

Dear God

I trust that You will put the right people on my path and that Your favor will cause me to be extremely fruitful.

Notes

Done
Wrong

REST WELL KNOWING THAT GOD WILL NOT ALLOW A WEAPON TO PROSPER NO MATTER WHO FORMS IT AGAINST YOU.

Sometimes it is a hard truth to accept, but it is often the people closest to you who can do the most damage. The people with whom you have to deal on some level, whether you work with them, you are married to them, or are related to them. These people distract you, stress you and test your faith in ways you didn't know were possible. The harder you try, the more they push the limits of your patience. But now you know better and realize you are not going to block your blessings because of someone else's foolishness. You know that God's grace really is sufficient for you to ignore them, and that God knows all too well that the people who can do the most harm are close enough to kiss you. So Rest Well knowing that regardless of how close or familiar the source may be, God will protect you and will not let what is being formed against you, defeat you.

"What shall we say about such wonderful things as these? If God is for us, who can ever be against us?" (Romans 8:31, NLT).

Dear God

I thank You that no weapon formed against me will harm me regardless of how familiar the source is.

Notes

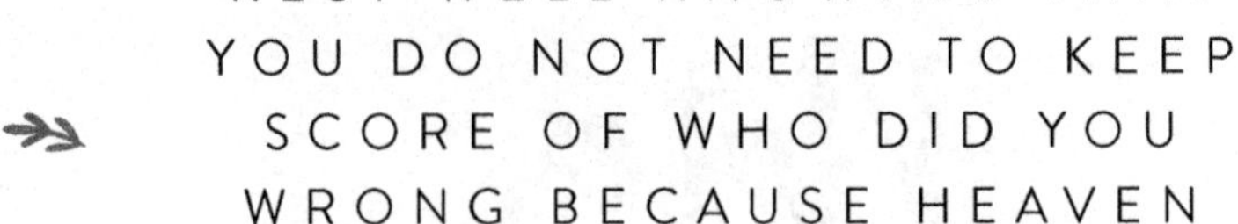

REST WELL KNOWING THAT YOU DO NOT NEED TO KEEP SCORE OF WHO DID YOU WRONG BECAUSE HEAVEN HAS A FULL ACCOUNTING.

Sometimes you rob yourself of your peace by what you are holding on to. You have a record of every wrong that was done, every offense you have experienced. You are secretly watching, wishing, and waiting for them to get what they deserve. Your feelings tell you that you can't move on or find closure until you know that their wrongs have been exposed and they paid for what they did. But now you know better and you have come to yourself and you realize that God says you have mourned long enough. It is time to move forward by faith. This isn't even your battle, it belongs to the Lord. So Rest Well knowing that you don't have to worry or concern yourself with what happened, heaven has a full accounting of everything, and when God sets the table for you in front of your enemies, He knows exactly who is on the invite list.

"And He pays even greater action to you, down to the last detail-even numbering the hairs on your head! So don't be intimidated by all this bully talk" (Luke 12:7, The Message).

Dear God

I trust You completely because You love me enough to number the hairs on my head. You know everything that has happened and that's all that matters.

Notes

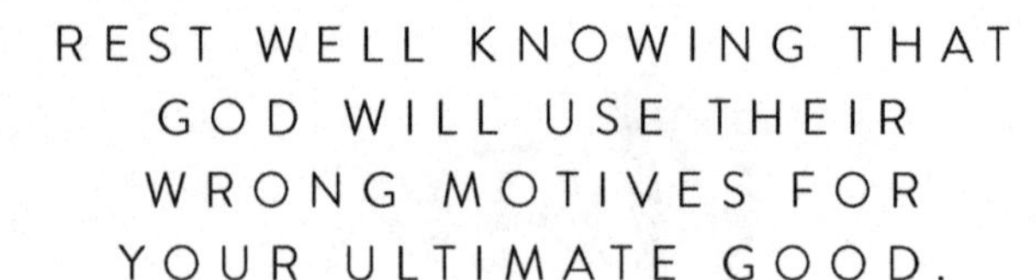

REST WELL KNOWING THAT GOD WILL USE THEIR WRONG MOTIVES FOR YOUR ULTIMATE GOOD.

Sometimes you get sidetracked on your faith walk because of the negative actions of other people. You discover that they had the wrong motive, and it sends you straight into an emotional hurricane. You are trying to understand why they had ill-intentions and you end up squandering your talents just because of what someone else did. The voice of doubt comes along and convinces you that somehow God's promises are subject to what was done to you. But now you know better and realize that shaking the dust off your feet and moving on is always the best response to a bad experience. You know that you don't need to understand why they did it because foolishness never has a valid reason. So Rest Well knowing that in spite of them having the wrong motives, God will still use it for your ultimate good.

"But I, the Lord, search all hearts and examine secret motives. I give all people their due rewards, according to what their actions deserve" (Jeremiah 17:10, NLT).

Dear God

I will take the focus off the wrong motives of others and keep my heart tuned toward the goodness You have planned for me.

Notes

REST WELL KNOWING THAT THE PEOPLE WHO ADDED FUEL TO YOUR FIRE DON'T KNOW THAT YOU'RE FIREPROOF.

Sometimes it seems so hard to understand why certain people seem to delight in your disappointment and would secretly celebrate your downfall. It's like they took a page out of the book of Job and are treating you with contempt just like his friends did. It causes you to doubt not only your ability to win, but God's willingness to bless you. But now you know better and realize that whatever people think you did wrong, God knows the truth and He will make things right. You know that God's amazing plan for your life will not be stopped by someone who clearly doesn't know you are more than a conqueror. So Rest Well knowing that the people who wanted to see you crash and burn are about to realize that God is with you in the fire and you are coming out stronger, wiser and fireproof.

"All the important people, the government leaders and king's counselors, gathered around to examine them and discovered that the fire hadn't so much as touched the three men-not a hair singed, not a scorch mark on their clothes, not even the smell of fire on them" (Daniel 3:27, The Message).

Dear God

I thank You that whatever fire I go through You will bring me through it and I will be better than ever without any residue or smoke smell.

Notes

REST WELL KNOWING THAT THEY THINK IT'S YOUR LOSS BUT THEY DON'T KNOW YOU'RE COUNTING IT ALL AS JOY.

Sometimes you get passed over, someone walks away, and the relationship you counted on has counted you out. You thought it was a long-term situation, but it became a short-term season. Your feelings are issuing invitations for your pity party and your critics and naysayers are preparing the eulogy for the desires of your heart. Eventually the voice of doubt convinces you that your blessing was connected to the person who left and that happiness is only something you used to know. But now you know better and realize that anything that left wasn't part of your promise. God's pruning isn't pitiful, it's powerful! You know that God will remove mediocrity to bless you with His best. So Rest Well knowing that the people who walked away may think it's your loss, but they don't know you are counting it all as joy because their leaving made room for God's best.

"Every desirable and beneficial gift comes out of heaven. The gifts are rivers of light cascading down from the Father of Light. There is nothing deceitful in God, nothing two-faced nothing fickle" (James 1:17, The Message).

Dear God

I will no longer attach my joy to a past relationship but will instead look to You as my Source for everything good and perfect.

Notes

REST WELL KNOWING THAT GOD WILL CAUSE YOU TO PROSPER IN SPITE OF WHO IS SCHEMING AGAINST YOU.

Sometimes you get so discouraged when you find out that there are people working against you, and they do not have your best interest at heart. It's as if someone has accepted the enemy's mission by working overtime to be a real thorn in your side. The voice of doubt tells you they are the giant that you can't slay. But now you know better and realize that regardless of who doesn't have your best interest at heart, God is still giving you the desires of your heart. Jacob's story is an example of the power of God's favor because the more Laban schemed against Jacob, the less he accomplished, showing that negative schemes are no match for your supernatural God. So Rest Well knowing that you have the favor of God on your side and anyone scheming against you will actually be used to bless you.

"He frustrates the plans of schemers so the work of their hands will not succeed" (Job 5:12, NLT).

Dear God

I will remain secure in the knowledge that a scheming thorn in my side will not stand because I have You on my side.

Notes

REST WELL KNOWING THAT TRUSTING IN GOD'S RESTORATION IS SO MUCH SWEETER THAN SEEKING REVENGE.

Sometimes no matter how Christian you are, in the face of someone doing you wrong, you want to get back at them. Your emotions get involved and you are determined to see them pay for what they did to you. In the secret place of your thoughts, you consider all the ways you could seek revenge. You don't even want to move forward because you want a front row seat to watch them pay for your pain. But now you know better and realize that God is fighting your battles and He will deliver your enemy into your hands. You know that vengeance belongs to Him and He will repay generously. So Rest Well knowing that you are blessed, in spite of what they have done and you don't need to waste your time seeking revenge, but pray for them and let them reap their harvest from the negative seeds they have sown.

"For we know the One who said, 'I will take revenge. I will pay them back.' He also said, 'The Lord will judge His own people'" (Hebrews 10:30, NLT).

Dear God

I am committed to living in Your perfect will and I know that revenge is not part of Your plan. I trust You to make right any wrong that has been done.

Notes

REST WELL KNOWING THAT THEIR WRONG DOES NOT INTERFERE WITH GOD'S GOOD PLANS.

Sometimes in the face of hurt, betrayal, or disappointment it is hard to keep your eyes on the prize. Your feelings convince you that it is impossible to move forward without an apology, without closure, or without a full-admission of how much their actions have impacted you. Eventually you get so consumed by what they did, you lose sight of what God promised. But now you know better and realize that God's good plan is not subject to the behavior of others. The word of God is evidence that even in the face of trickery, lies, and wrong-doings, God is still going to have His way. You know that what you're feeling has absolutely nothing to do with what God is capable of doing on your behalf. So Rest Well knowing that whomever did you wrong is about to become a distant memory, because God's great plans are your ever-present reality.

"And my tongue will talk of your righteous help all the day long, for they have been put to shame and disappointed who sought to do me hurt" (Psalm 71:24, ESV).

Dear God

I forget anything negative that was done and remember all of the benefits that come from trusting in You in all things.

Notes

God's
Plans

REST WELL KNOWING THAT WHEN YOU KEEP GOD AT THE CENTER OF YOUR PLANS, THE DEVIL CAN'T GET INTO YOUR DETAILS.

Sometimes you can get so focused on every little detail of what you are trying to accomplish that you lose sight of the large vision God gave you. There is very little joy for your journey because you are too busy worrying and stressing. You are relying on your own strength while growing weary by overthinking everything, by considering every possibility of what could go wrong. But now you know better and realize there is a better way. God said you don't need to rely on your own abilities, you just need to follow His instructions. You may be growing weary trying to figure it all out, but the joy God gives you is your strength. So Rest Well knowing that the amazing plan God has for you will come to pass and with Jesus at the center of your life, the enemy has no authority over the details.

"Commit your actions to the LORD, and your plans will succeed" (Proverbs 16:13, NLT).

Dear God

I embrace Your joy as my source of strength and I know that You have authority over all the details for the plans You have for me.

Notes

REST WELL KNOWING THAT YOUR CIRCUMSTANCE DOESN'T CHANGE GOD'S PLAN.

Sometimes you are not walking with a purpose; not pursuing God's best or even believing for better simply because your temporary circumstance is calling the shots. You allow what you are experiencing in the moment to dictate all of your decision-making and your level of faith. Truth be told, your doubt has nothing to do with God and everything to do with what you are going through. But now you know better and realize that the moment you start leaning on your own understanding is when you start tripping. You know that if your situation was to suddenly change, God's promises remain the same -- yesterday, today, and forever. Your level of faith is not about what you're going through, it is about what God has already done for you. So Rest Well knowing that your temporary circumstances are about to become a distant memory because God's amazing plan for your life remains the same.

"I'm convinced: You can do anything and everything. Nothing and no one can upset your plans" (Job 42:2 The Message).

Dear God

I thank You that Your plans are steadfast and consistent in spite of my temporary situation, Your long-term plan for my life will succeed.

Notes

REST WELL KNOWING THAT IT MAY NOT HAVE WORKED OUT THE WAY YOU THOUGHT, BUT GOD HAS SOMETHING BETTER THAN YOU COULD IMAGINE.

One of the hardest things to do when you walk by faith is to keep trusting God when things don't go your way. You had a really good idea of what your life should look like at this point and yet your reality looks nothing like what you envisioned. The voice of doubt tells you that God is great for your eternal plans, but not much help for your current earthly situation. But now you know better and realize that in spite of what you had planned, God has a more amazing plan. You know that you don't really want the limited life you thought, you want the life that God promised would be beyond all you could think. So Rest Well knowing that things may not have worked out the way you thought, but that is because God has something mind-blowing that is better than you could have imagined.

"Now to Him who is able to do immeasurably more than all we ask or imagine, according to His power that is at work within us" (Ephesians 3:20, NIV).

Dear God

I exchange my disappointment for Your promises knowing that what You have planned for me is better than I could ever imagine.

Notes

REST WELL KNOWING THAT GOD IS NOT INTIMIDATED BY WHERE HE FOUND YOU BECAUSE HE KNOWS WHERE HE IS TAKING YOU.

Sometimes the only thing standing between you and a brighter tomorrow is the fact that you continue to rehearse the past. You let what you used to be prophesize what you can become. It puts you in a holding-pattern where you have left behind the wrong people, habits or situations, but you are too intimidated to go forward into your promise. The voice of doubt causes confusion and interrupts your ability to believe for the better. But now you know better and realize that God knows the end from the beginning and He knew exactly where He would find you and what He had planned for you. God is not overwhelmed by the things you don't understand because His thoughts are so far beyond your ability to conceive His awesomeness. So Rest Well knowing that where God found you is irrelevant because of where He is taking you to fulfill His good plans.

"O Lord, I will honor and praise your name, for you are my God. You do such wonderful things! You planned them long ago, and now you have accomplished them" (Isaiah 25:1, NLT).

Dear God

I release the guilt and shame from my past so that I can fully embrace Your plan and Your promise for my life.

Notes

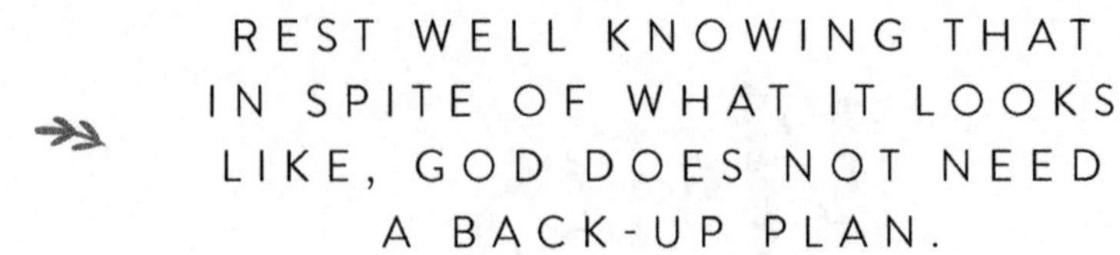

Sometimes you can pay so much undue attention to the critics and "Negative Nancys" in your life that you begin to question God's ability to do what He said. You know that He has a good plan for your life but you don't know how He is going to make it happen. So you start negotiating with the voice of doubt, trying to come up with a workable compromise. But now you know better and realize that God can do everything but fail, and when you take a leap of faith, God provides the safety net. You know that the only reason your critics keep talking about a "plan B" is because they can't comprehend God's amazing "plan A." So Rest Well knowing that you can ignore the naysayers because God's plans will always prevail and He is more than able to fulfill all of His promises.

"We humans keep brainstorming options and plans, but God's purpose prevails" (Proverbs 19:21, The Message).

Dear God

I am not going to stress about a back-up plan and instead I will put my energy into trusting Your plan.

Notes

REST WELL KNOWING THAT GOD'S INSTRUCTIONS MAY NOT BE LOGICAL, BUT THEY WILL ALWAYS PROVE BENEFICIAL.

Sometimes you seek God for a serious challenge that demands a divine solution. You needed a breakthrough yesterday in order to face tomorrow. You start wondering if God really understands you, or even knows the depth of your upset or the seriousness of your situation. The voice of doubt tells you that you need to just suffer until you find a solution that makes sense. But now you know better and realize that God has a proven track record of unusual methods. Marching in silence, dipping in dirty water, or putting mud on your eyes to correct your vision didn't really make sense, but they didn't need to make sense because they made way for God to do the supernatural. So Rest Well knowing that it is okay if you don't understand God's methods to solve your problem, because you will absolutely recognize when He does the miraculous in your life.

"For the message of the cross is foolishness to those who are perishing, but to us who are being saved it is the power of God" (1 Corinthians 1:18, NIV).

Dear God

I am fully persuaded that faith begins when my logic runs out and Your solutions don't need to make sense because they bring about results.

Notes

REST WELL KNOWING THAT GOD'S FAVOR IS NOT RANDOM, IT IS VERY INTENTIONAL TOWARD YOU.

Sometimes you look around and wonder why it seems like everyone is being blessed but you. You see people getting promotions, having great relationships, and living the desires of their heart. The voice of doubt answers you by humanizing God and exploiting all of your perceived deficits, as if saying "You're not smart enough, educated enough, or good enough." Eventually your worth begins to diminish based upon the wrong information. But now you know better and realize that from heaven's perspective you are priceless! God made you complete, lacking nothing. It is foolish to count someone else's blessings because God has so many blessings prepared for you and God rewards faith when you are in doubt. So Rest Well knowing that God's favor is not some random occurrence, it is part of His Master plan for you to live in His exceeding and abundant blessings because you trust Him with everything.

"May He grant your heart's desires and make all your plans succeed" (Psalm 20:4, NLT).

Dear God

I believe You have already prepared the desires of my heart and Your good plan is succeeding in my life.

Notes

REST WELL KNOWING THAT GOD'S AMAZING PLAN WILL ALWAYS PREVAIL OVER YOUR PROBLEM.

Sometimes it is so hard to believe in your promise when all you can see are your problems: what you don't have, what didn't work out, and who isn't here for you. The voice of doubt is doing major damage to your ability to remain positive. Eventually you start to see your situation through the lens of fear and it doesn't look good. Somehow what seemed like a small problem is now looking more like a giant problem. But now you know better and realize that God does not need you to have all the answers, He wants you to trust Him as the Solution. You are going to stay positive and remain hopeful simply because you know God is so faithful; the problem becomes irrelevant because God is the Master problem-solver. So Rest Well knowing that your temporary problems are not going to interrupt God's amazing plan.

"The Lord of Heaven's Armies has sworn this oath: 'It will all happen as I have planned. It will be as I have decided.'" (Isaiah 14:24, NLT).

Dear God

I thank You for the ability to look beyond my problems and see Your promises and trust Your plan.

Notes

Confidence

REST WELL KNOWING THAT YOU CAN WALK OUT OF YOUR SITUATION WITH CONFIDENCE BECAUSE GOD IS STANDING WATCH OVER HIS WORD.

Sometimes you have to walk through a difficult situation and you start to doubt if you will ever come out on the other side. It starts to become a real struggle to put one foot in front of the other wondering when you will ever see the manifestation of your promise. You know what God's word says, but your feelings are telling you to give up, it's too hard and maybe you just misunderstood what God said in the first place. But now you know better and realize that God said all things are possible, even when they are not always easy; you are a winner not a quitter. You know that speaking God's word breathes life into any situation, and on the other side of victory your faith walk will seem like a cake walk. So Rest Well knowing that God protects and honors His word to make sure you inherit your promise.

"Then the LORD said to me, 'You have seen well, for I am watching over my word to perform it.'" (Jeremiah 1:12, ESV).

Dear God

I will walk out of my situation with confidence because I know Your word will not return void and it will accomplish what You please.

Notes

REST WELL KNOWING THAT THE REASON YOU CAN WAIT ON GOD WITH PATIENCE IS BECAUSE HE HAS A PROVEN TRACK RECORD OF PERFORMING ON HIS WORD.

Sometimes you get so impatient with what has not happened yet, you grow weary of waiting and become a magnet for unbelief. You look around and think that surely if God cared, if God were going to come through, then He should have done so by now. The voice of doubt fuels your frustration and tells you it has been long enough, time's up and you need to take matters into your own hands. But now you know better and realize when you wait on God with a renewed mind, He will renew your strength. You know that taking matters into your own hands gives birth to your problems and you would rather wait on God to give birth to your promise. So Rest Well knowing that you can be fully persuaded and confident in believing for better because God has a proven track record of performing on His word.

"For the vision is yet for the appointed time; it testifies about the end and will not lie. Though it delays, wait for it, since it will certainly come and not be late" (Habakkuk 2:3, The Holman Bible).

Dear God

I wait with patience and confidence because You have shown Yourself more than able to honor Your word and deliver on Your promise.

Notes

REST WELL KNOWING YOU CAN FACE THE FACTS WITH CONFIDENCE BECAUSE YOU KNOW THE TRUTH.

Sometimes you want to bury your head in the sand regarding your situation and you wish you could just anesthetize yourself to what is going on around you. It may be a bad medical report, a broken relationship, or a financial challenge, but you procrastinate on dealing with it, instead thinking and hoping that if you simply ignore it, then maybe it will go away. The major problem is the company you keep that tells you to face the facts and prepare for the worst. But now you know better and realize that God said to be strong and courageous because He is always with you, and He gave you His peace so that you should not be troubled or afraid. So Rest Well knowing that you can face the facts with confidence because you are standing on God's truth that says you can overcome anything and prosper in all things.

"The righteous person faces many troubles, but the Lord comes to the rescue each time" (Psalm 34:19, NLT).

Dear God

I don't deny the facts of my life, I just deny their power over me because Your word is the ultimate authority.

Notes

REST WELL KNOWING THAT WHEN YOU SEEK FIRST THE KINGDOM YOU DON'T NEED TO LOOK FOR APPROVAL FROM ANYONE ELSE.

Sometimes your feelings will cause you to take your eye off of the prize and start seeking the approval of others. You want someone to be the cheerleader to celebrate your obedience, applaud your faith move, or agree with your faith decision. Your negative thoughts form a partnership with doubt and now you need acceptance and permission from others in order to trust God and pursue the desires of your heart. But now you know better and realize that you don't need anyone to celebrate or agree with your obedience because you have already been given God's authority. So Rest Well knowing that you are seeking first God's Kingdom and it is not a democracy; He does not need permission or popular opinion to bless you beyond all you could ask or think.

"Obviously, I'm not trying to win the approval of people, but of God. If people pleasing were my goal, I wouldn't be Christ's servant" (Galatians 1:10, NLT).

Dear God

I will put You first in everything and seek to be pleasing to You by trusting in Your word and standing on Your promise.

Notes

REST WELL KNOWING THAT WHAT YOU LEARNED IN YOUR STRUGGLE WILL BE JUST WHAT YOU NEED TO OCCUPY YOUR PROMISE.

Sometimes it's hard to make sense of what you're going through and you feel that even though you are doing everything right, you still can't seem to get the right result. It seems like the more you try to have faith, the more things seem to come against you. Negative thoughts take over and you start murmuring and complaining while wondering if God is really going to make good on His promise. But now you know better and are confident that God is strategic and anything you are going through isn't to punish you, but to prepare you. He doesn't just take you into your promise, He equips you to occupy and flourish. You can stop complaining and start thanking Him for what He has planned. So Rest Well knowing that what you think is your difficult place is really your preparation place because God always makes good on His promises.

"But blessed are those who trust in the Lord and have made the Lord their hope and confidence" (Jeremiah 17:7, NLT).

Dear God

I trust that any struggle I'm experiencing is making me stronger and wiser and preparing me to occupy my promise.

Notes

REST WELL AND BE CONFIDENT IN KNOWING THAT GOD IS FAITHFUL EVEN IN YOUR UNFAMILIAR PLACE.

Sometimes you stay stuck and settle for less because you have allowed your emotions to worship your comfort. The voice of doubt has convinced you that somehow God is limited by geography and can only bless you and keep you in your familiar place. You want to experience the desires of your heart, but you don't want to step out on faith. You have wondered why God doesn't just enlarge your territory from inside your comfort zone. But now you know better and realize that anything worth having is worth the trust in God. To place limits on God is foolishness when you consider His faithfulness. On the other side of victory, you will realize that comfort was overrated in comparison to your promise. So Rest Well knowing that you can step out of your familiar place with confidence because even when your situation is unfamiliar, God has already prepared the way.

"God is striding ahead of you. He's right there with you. He won't let you down; He won't leave you. Don't be intimidated. Don't worry" (Deuteronomy 31:8, The Message).

Dear God

I refuse to allow my familiar place to keep me from my promised place and I'm going to trust You with all confidence even in the midst of uncertainty.

Notes

REST WELL KNOWING THAT CONFIDENTLY WAITING ON GOD ISN'T PASSIVE, IT'S POWERFUL.

Sometimes you are so jaded by popular culture that you start to wonder if faith and patience is for weak-minded people who lack the courage and confidence to pursue their dreams. Waiting is an excuse for those who will never accomplish much because the real movers and shakers are out there taking matters into their own hands, getting it done and making boss moves. But now you know better and realize that what you believe is stronger than anything in popular culture. You know that waiting on God isn't about doing nothing, it's about trusting God with everything while you prepare for His best. You are much greater than a mover and a shaker, because you are a conqueror and an overcomer. So Rest Well knowing that you can wait on God with confidence because it is not a passive position, it is a powerful position.

"Yet I am confident I will see the Lord's goodness while I adhere in the land of the living. Wait patiently for the Lord. Be brave and courageous. Yes, wait patiently for the Lord" (Psalm 27: 13-14, NLT).

Dear God

I know the most powerful thing I can do on my faith walk is to wait with confidence and patience with great expectation of Your goodness.

Notes

REST WELL KNOWING THAT YOUR ENEMY IS PERSISTENT BUT NOT POWERFUL.

Sometimes it seems like the enemy is hitting you so hard that surely this enemy has the upper hand. Truth be told, it feels like your enemy is in relentless pursuit and is throwing a sucker-punch to the gut. You are stumbling, trying to catch your breath, find your footing as your emotions come undone. You are fighting against the enemy of unbelief, and you are convinced that what is coming at you is far more powerful than you are. But now you know better and realize that nobody has the upper hand on you because you have placed your battle in God's supernatural hands. You may get knocked down, but with faith you are bouncing right back. You know that God already destroyed the enemy's power and now that enemy has no authority in your life. So Rest Well knowing that the enemy may be persistent but is no match for the power of God inside of you.

"Finally, be strong in the Lord and in His mighty power" (Ephesians 6:10, NIV).

Dear God

I am confident that the enemy has no authority in my life and he may try to be persistent but he is no match for Your mighty power.

Notes

God's Faithfulness

REST WELL KNOWING THAT GOD IS TOO FAITHFUL FOR YOU TO TAKE TODAY'S FOOLISHNESS INTO TOMORROW'S NEW MERCIES.

Sometimes it is so tempting to hold on to an upset or an offense by someone. You feel completely justified in your anger towards them because they were completely in the wrong and you are completely confident that you are right. Your emotions tell you that forgiveness is a good idea, but not yet. You feel that you deserve to marinate in the upset of what they did for a while, after all, feeling justified sets the stage for hosting a fabulous pity-party. But now you know better and realize that no offense is worth blocking your blessing, and forgiveness is not given to help the offender, but it is given to position you for God's underserved grace. You know that you have no need of a pity-party because you are planning a victory celebration. So Rest Well knowing that God is far too faithful and His promises are too close at hand for you to use the foolishness of today to hinder the blessings of tomorrow.

"The faithful love of the Lord never ends! His mercies never cease. Great is His faithfulness; His mercies begin afresh each morning" (Lamentations 3:22-23, NLT).

Dear God

I release any offense or upset of today and look forward to the new mercies You have prepared for me in the morning.

Notes

REST WELL KNOWING THAT GOD IS FAR MORE FAITHFUL AND STRATEGIC THAN YOUR CRITICS CAN COMPREHEND.

Sometimes the well-meaning naysayers in your life believe they are being helpful when they tell you to give up. They tell you it's an impossible situation with the odds stacked completely against you and that "common sense" dictates that it is ridiculous for you to keep speaking life to a hopeless cause. You don't know how your situation is going to turn around, or how you are going to break through and come out on the other side of the situation. It seems like throwing in the towel is your last resort and the best option. But now you know better and realize that faith is not your last resort, it is the final word. That common sense has its place but it can never replace uncommon favor and divine strategy. So Rest Well knowing that the odds are not stacked against you when God is standing with you and He is so much more faithful than your critics can comprehend.

"If we are faithless, He remains faithful-for He cannot deny Himself" (2 Timothy 2:13, ESV).

Dear God

Forgive me for doubting your faithfulness and I am truly grateful that regardless of my lack of faith, You never give up on me.

Notes

REST WELL KNOWING THAT GOD IS TOO FAITHFUL FOR YOU TO LET FEAR HOLD YOU BACK.

Sometimes you dim your light and dial down your greatness simply because you accepted advice from the voice of doubt. You believe God for better yet there is something that keeps you from getting out of the boat. Your emotions rationalize it with things such as: the timing isn't right, your finances aren't ready, or you need help from someone on whom you cannot count. But now you know better and understand that God did not give you the spirit of fear but the spirit of power with a "can do" mindset. You know that you are walking by faith and fear has no place on your journey. God said you can boldly proclaim that He is your help and you have nothing to fear. So Rest Well knowing that God has brought you too far and He is far too faithful for you to miss your blessings simply because you let fear hold you back.

"I prayed to the Lord, and He answered me. He freed me from all my fears" (Psalm 34:4, NLT).

Dear God

I know that fear loses its power when I make trusting in You my priority and elevate my faith above anything I may be feeling.

Notes

REST WELL KNOWING THAT THE STRUGGLE IS REAL BUT GOD IS STILL FAITHFUL.

Sometimes you are so bombarded by bad news that struggling can seem like the new normal. Everywhere you look, people are having a hard time, barely making it from day-to-day. Between social media, the news, and reality television, it's a wonder you have any peace or hope for the future. The voice of doubt will convince you to settle beneath your promise because what you're trying to accomplish is too difficult. But now you know better and understand why God told you to guard your heart and take every thought captive. If God didn't say it, you're not giving it a second thought, instead you are speaking what you believe and letting God's word take authority over your situation. So Rest Well knowing that to the world, the struggle is very real, but you are more than a conqueror and God is still more than faithful.

"Know this: God, your God, is God indeed, a God you can depend upon. He keeps His covenant of loyal love with those who love Him and observe His commandments for a thousand generations" (Deuteronomy 7:9, The Message).

Dear God

I reject the world's definition of struggle because I know You called me to Your good purpose and Your faithfulness will sustain me.

Notes

REST WELL KNOWING THAT GOD IS SO FAITHFUL IN SPITE OF HOW YOU ARE FEELING.

Sometimes when you are believing big, it's hard to discern between your faith and your feelings. You know what you believe but your emotions can have such a stronghold on you that they get elevated above your faith. Before you know it, you're worshipping your feelings and your faith is expected to follow along. You make an emotional decision and sprinkle a little God on it hoping for the best. But now you know better and realize your emotions do not have the capacity to understand the faithfulness of God. You know that you walk by faith, not by a feeling, because God can do the miraculous and you won't feel a thing until you arrive on the other side of victory. So Rest Well knowing that the only currency of the Kingdom is faith and God is working in your favor in spite of how you are feeling.

"Your faithfulness endures to all generations; you have established the earth, and it stands fast" (Psalm 119:90, ESV).

Dear God

I exchange my feelings for Your faithfulness knowing that You are always working everything in my favor no matter how I feel.

Notes

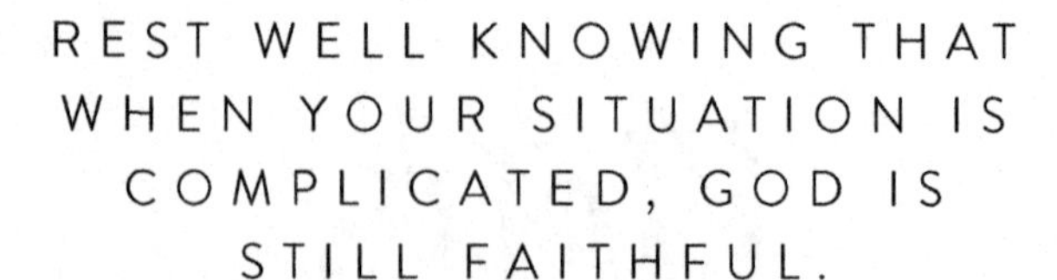

Sometimes you get overwhelmed by the tough decisions of life, the fork in the road, the what-comes-next seasons of life. It seems like there are no good options and whether you go left or right, neither will work out in your favor. You struggle to find clarity, but everywhere you look there is chaos and confusion. The voice of doubt exploits your uncertainty by saying your situation is "complicated" and it causes you to put a limit on what is possible. Eventually you start to think complicated means fatal and it causes serious unbelief. But now you know better and realize that your steps are ordered and God will command a blessing whichever way you go. You know that chaos is a lie, because God's word brings clarity and truth. So Rest Well knowing that your situation isn't a complication, it is an opportunity for God to show Himself faithful.

"The temptations in your life are no different from what others experience. And God is faithful. He will not allow the temptation to be more than you can stand. When you are tempted, He will show you a way out so that you can endure" (1 Corinthians 10:13, NLT).

Dear God

I know that in spite of how complicated I think my situation is, Your faithfulness brings clarity and You already have a plan to sort things out for my good.

Notes

REST WELL KNOWING THAT GOD IS SO FAITHFUL THAT HE WILL COMMAND A BLESSING UPON YOUR DEPARTURE.

Sometimes a situation comes to an end and it is time to move on in a different direction, whether it is a new job, a new relationship, even a new city. The challenge is in the unknown. You know God's best is available, but you don't quite know what that looks like or where it can be found. Truth be told, you want to be obedient but thoughts of doubt and unbelief seem to overwhelm you. But now you know better and realize that God always brings you out better than you went in and the greatest blessings come when God takes you in a new direction. You have nothing to be overwhelmed about because God has purposed you to be an overcomer. So Rest Well knowing that God is so faithful that when He calls you to leave, He will command a blessing upon your departure.

"You will be blessed when you come in and blessed when you go out" (Deuteronomy 28:6, NIV).

Dear God

I know that a dead-end or a fork in the road doesn't matter because You have already prepared my blessings regardless of a new direction.

Notes

REST WELL KNOWING THAT GOD'S RESOURCES FOLLOW YOUR FAITHFULNESS.

Sometimes you really want to achieve your goals and commit to your purpose. You try to step out on faith but then you get stuck worrying about what you don't have: not enough time, not enough money, not enough strength. You really want to live the life of your dreams, but you don't know if you have what it takes. Bravery and the ability to take a risk of faith aren't in you. You feel that it would be better to have the provision in-hand before you set out on your journey. But now you know better and realize that divine provision is always where God told you to go, not where you decided to stay. You know that a risk of faith brings about the best rewards. So Rest Well knowing that when you step out on faith, God has already gone before you and the richness of His resources are leading the way.

"So Abraham called the name of that place, 'The Lord will provide,' as it is said to this day, 'On the mount of the Lord it shall be provided.'" (Genesis 22:14, ESV).

Dear God

I will be obedient to Your direction knowing that if You have to bring water out of a rock or send bread into the wilderness, You will make sure I have all that I need.

Notes

Open Doors and New Opportunities

REST WELL KNOWING THAT YOU DO NOT NEED TO CHASE AFTER WHAT LEFT BECAUSE GOD'S FAVOR WILL FIND YOU.

Sometimes running after what left you looks like the most logical thing to do: that opportunity you missed, the relationship that didn't work out the way you wanted, or even the finances that seem to have gone astray. Popular culture tells you that the only way to have the life of your dreams is to spend every waking hour chasing after it. You are starting to feel like a hamster on a wheel, constantly running but not getting anywhere or accomplishing anything. But now you know better and realize that when you pursue God's purpose, you don't have to chase what wasn't meant to be caught. You know that you don't need to run like a hamster on a wheel, you can simply walk by faith because your steps are ordered. So Rest Well knowing that you don't need to chase anything that left, God's favor will find you and His blessings will overtake you.

"For whoever finds me finds life and receives favor from the Lord" (Proverbs 8:35, NLT).

Dear God

I am going to excuse myself from the rat race and just run the race You have set before me knowing that Your favor and blessings will overtake me.

Notes

REST WELL KNOWING THAT BEAUTIFUL NEW BEGINNINGS CAN BE BORN OUT OF AN UNHAPPY ENDING.

Sometimes it is so hard to see the newness that awaits you and the possibilities for your future simply because of something that did not work out the way you thought: the relationship that went south, the career advancement you expected but fell through, even that one thing you really prayed for that has not happened. The more you replay your steps in your mind, the more hardened and broken your heart becomes. Your feelings shift you into a place of unbelief and, truth be told, you do not expect much better than what you have already experienced. But now you know better and realize that you cannot pour new wine into old wineskins, and that some doors have to close in order to make room for what comes next. God works things for your good, not necessarily how you thought. So Rest Well knowing that what you thought was an unhappy ending is about to be revealed as your beautiful new beginning.

"Be alert, be present, I'm about to do something brand-new. It's bursting out! Don't you see it? There it is! I'm making a road through the desert, rivers in the badlands" (Isaiah 43:10, The Message).

Dear God

I trust You with any unhappy ending because I am fully persuaded that You have an amazing new beginning prepared for me.

Notes

REST WELL KNOWING THAT DIVINE PROMOTION COMES IN THE MOST UNUSUAL WAYS.

Sometimes it is hard to dream big and believe for better simply because you just do not see how it would be possible. Your situation says, "no way," and your circumstance is far from ideal. You cannot muster the strength to expect an upgrade when all you see looks like a downgrade and a step backward. Whatever hope you were trying to keep alive is on life-support and you are about ready to pull the plug. But now you know better and realize that you don't need to look around at your situation, you need to look up because that's from where your real help comes. You know that, just like Joseph, God will cause your oppressor to become your greatest opportunity. So Rest Well knowing that you may not know how God's going to do it, but divine promotion and open doors are your portion and they come in the most unusual ways.

"The warden had no more worries, because Joseph took care of everything. The Lord was with him and caused everything he did to succeed" (Genesis 39:23, NLT).

Dear God

I trust that even in the midst of a situation I didn't expect and don't understand, You will open doors in the most unexpected yet awesome ways.

Notes

REST WELL KNOWING THAT A MANUFACTURED PROBLEM IS NO MATCH FOR YOUR SUPERNATURAL GOD.

Sometimes your negative feelings actually manufacture the magnitude of your problem. Yes, you've had a setback, you've encountered an obstacle or faced disappointment. But now your emotions have made it larger than life: a mountain too high, a valley too deep or a wilderness too vast. You cannot think about living in your promised place because you are stuck in your difficult place. But now you know better and realize that a setback is the launching pad for a breakthrough. You know that mustard seed faith is more than enough to deal with any mountain, valley, or wilderness, and like David, what looks like an obstacle too great is really an opportunity too big to miss. So Rest Well knowing that negative emotions may try to manufacture the size of your problem but it is still no match for the supernatural power of your God.

"I am the Lord, the God of all mankind. Is anything too hard for me?" (Jeremiah 32:27, NIV).

Dear God

I will stop letting my emotions overdramatize my problem because I believe You will do the supernatural in my situation because nothing is too hard for You.

Notes

REST WELL KNOWING THAT A CLOSED DOOR IS IRRELEVANT BECAUSE YOU LIVE UNDER AN OPEN HEAVEN.

Sometimes you allow a closed door to cause you to take your eye off of the prize. You over-think what did not work out, you believe rejection is your portion, and that somehow you are being denied something that you really thought you deserved. Those well-meaning "Negative Nancys" in your life say that a closed door is the end of your story, as if God is now incapable of blessing you. But now you know better and realize that God doesn't withhold any good thing from you. It brings Him pleasure for you to live the glorious life He has planned. You know that man-made doors do not even phase the God who will easily bring down the walls. So Rest Well knowing that a closed door is so irrelevant to God because He purposed you to live under His open heaven.

"Then He said, 'I tell you the truth, you will see heaven open and the angels of God going up and down on the Son of Man, the one who is the stairway between heaven and earth'" (John 1:51, NLT).

Dear God

I will not let a closed door disrupt my faith because I know this is my season to live under Your open heaven of grace and blessings.

Notes

REST WELL KNOWING THAT DIVINE PROTECTION CAN COME BY WAY OF A CLOSED DOOR.

Sometimes your feelings become overly-invested in a closed door. You start thinking about what could have been if only things had gone your way, or if the relationship had worked out, or if the opportunity had been available to you. Eventually your emotions create an entire narrative full of regret and you resign yourself to think that surely God's favor is nowhere to be found in your life. But now you know better and realize that even when things don't work out, God is working for your good. You know that the eyes of your understanding are opened to the divine opportunities He has prepared for you. He is a stronghold in times of trouble, and watches over you to keep you from harm's way. So Rest Well knowing that from heaven's perspective, the door that did not open isn't denying you anything, it's keeping you from the wrong opportunity.

"I will give him the key to the house of David-the highest position in the royal court. When He opens doors, no one will be able to close them; when He closes doors, no one will able to open them" (Isaiah 22:22, NLT).

Dear God

I trust You with my closed door and open the eyes of my understanding to see the divine opportunities You have placed in my path.

Notes

REST WELL KNOWING THAT GOD USES ORDINARY SITUATIONS TO BRING ABOUT OUTSTANDING RESULTS.

Sometimes you are walking by faith but you have no clue how it's ever going to work in your favor. When you look around, your situation doesn't even resemble your promise and it feels like your faith walk has you set up to fail. It really bothers you that the dreams and goals you had for your life are not coming to fruition. To make matters worse, it's as if God is not giving you anything to work with in order to have the life you really want. But now you know better and realize that putting mud on your eyes or dipping in dirty water weren't much to go by, but they produced awesome results. You know that what looks like a set-up for failure is really the start-up of your turnaround. So Rest Well knowing that the ordinariness of your situation becomes your exceeding, abundant and extraordinary blessings.

"By faith these people overthrew kingdoms, ruled with justice, and received what God had promised them" (Hebrews 11:33, NLT).

Dear God

I believe by faith that You are turning my ordinary situation into extraordinary and outstanding results.

Notes

God's
Promises

REST WELL KNOWING THAT GOD'S PROMISES ARE STILL YES, IN SPITE OF WHO TOLD YOU NO.

It can be very difficult and discouraging when you hear the word NO. The word speaks of rejection, denial, and can even cause you to doubt that God is really on your side. Your confidence starts to erode and you are ready to climb back into the boat and retreat to your comfort zone. But now you know better and realize that NO is not fatal, it is actually not even relevant. Because what God promised will not be denied by a closed door, a missed opportunity, or even a loved-one who turned away from you. Your steps are ordered and God's word is true; therefore, NO is not your portion. In fact, the next time someone tells you NO, simply ask a different question. So Rest Well knowing that if someone told you NO, you don't have to accept it as the last word because God's promises are still YES and AMEN.

"For no matter how many promises God has made, they are "Yes" in Christ. And so through Him the "Amen" is spoken by us to the glory of God" (2 Corinthians 1:20, NIV).

Dear God

I speak life over my promises and stand firmly in Your YES in spite of who or what told me NO.

Notes

REST WELL KNOWING THAT YOUR PROMISE WAS ESTABLISHED BEFORE YOUR PROBLEM EVEN EXISTED.

Sometimes your problems can take center stage in your life and cause you to take your eye off the prize. Your negative thoughts are meditating on the problem so much so that it causes your feelings to give higher priority to what you are going through more so than what God promised you. Eventually your heart is left unguarded and in creeps all manner of unbelief. Your promise seemed like a good idea, but perhaps God didn't factor in that you would be faced with such problems. But now you know better and realize that God knows the end from the beginning, so your problem didn't catch Him off guard. Your problems are only temporary, but God's promises are eternal and from heaven's perspective whatever you perceive as a challenge is already solved. So Rest Well knowing that your problem is completely irrelevant to the great blessings God has already prepared of you.

"Let's keep a firm grip on the promises that keep us going. He always keeps His word" (Hebrews 10:23, The Message).

Dear God

I trust in Your promises more than I trust in any problems I may be experiencing because I know Your word is true and You are faithful.

Notes

REST WELL KNOWING THAT STANDING ON YOUR PROMISE IS YOUR BEST BOSS MOVE.

Sometimes you can go to God believing He can help with the big things, but you still feel like you need to prove yourself by taking drastic action. You see that other people are succeeding, living the life of their dreams and just outright winning. You want to "do" something because seeking, waiting and trusting do not produce any visible appearance of progress. The voice of doubt tells you to do more, to take matters into your own hands, and to show proof that you are making moves and making it happen. But now you know better and realize that God rewards those with radical faith, that every good thing imaginable is added into your life when you seek Him first, and that waiting on God is not a matter of doing nothing, it is a matter of preparing for His best. So Rest Well knowing that God is so faithful that standing on your promise will prove to be your best BOSS move yet.

"The One who called you is completely dependable. If He said it, He'll do it!" (1 Thessalonians 5:24, The Message).

Dear God

Thank You for renewing my strength so I can stand patiently on Your word and wait on Your best with hopeful expectation because I know You are faithful and You always honor Your promises.

Notes

REST WELL KNOWING THAT YOUR IMPERFECTIONS DO NOT DISQUALIFY YOU FROM GOD'S AMAZING PROMISES.

Sometimes the thing that holds you back is one of the greatest tricks of the enemy, the lie of perfection. Since you profess to have faith, then your life should be perfect. You waste time worrying about what is wrong with you instead of receiving God's grace to try and get it right. Naysayers criticize and confuse you by questioning your faith when your life isn't perfect. But now you know better and realize that God does not require your perfection, He wants you to live in His perfect will. You know that His grace is more than sufficient to cover any of your imperfections. While your critics are busy checking your image and looking for perfection, God is searching your heart and honoring your faith. So Rest Well knowing that your promises have already been prepared and you don't need to be perfect in order to stretch forth your faith and receive blessings.

"No unbelief made him waver concerning the promise of God, but he grew strong in his faith as he gave glory to God, fully convinced that God was able to do what he had promised" (Romans 4:20-21, ESV).

Dear God

I am at peace with my imperfections and with Your grace I am growing more like You and I will experience Your abundant promises.

Notes

REST WELL KNOWING THAT ANYTHING YOU LOSE IN YOUR STRUGGLE HAS MADE ROOM FOR WHAT'S BEEN PROMISED.

Sometimes the hardest thing about experiencing your next level of promises come from being weighed down with things that were never meant to travel with you. You are clinging tightly to a very poor resemblance of God's best, believing that something is better than nothing, so you settle for less and justify it as being humble. But now you know better and realize that God gives good and perfect gifts, not some "make-do, second-rate" blessing. You know that He is still in the pruning business and even though you may have been willing to take what was available, God's plans for you is to have what has been promised, and He will remove the wrong things from your life that are distracting you from His very best. So Rest Well knowing that God has a great plan for your next level promises and what you have lost was not personal, it is actually purposeful.

"Because you got a double dose of trouble and more than your share of contempt, Your inheritance in the land will be doubled and your joy go on forever" (Isaiah 61:7, The Message).

Dear God

I will not lose hope because of what I lost during my struggle because You just enlarged my capacity to receive Your promises.

Notes

REST WELL KNOWING THAT YOU DO NOT NEED TO WAIT FOR GOD TO SHOW UP IN YOUR SITUATION BECAUSE HE IS ALREADY THERE.

Sometimes you find yourself bombarding heaven and begging God to please come into your circumstance. You have humanized God and treated Him like He has a full schedule and may not have time to come through for you. The voice of doubt takes undue advantage of you by using your impatience to fuel your unbelief. You are growing weary in the process of waiting and you start wondering if you need to just take matters into your own hands. But now you know better and realize that God never leaves you or forsakes you whether you are in the pit, the fire or the lion's den. You know that He has an appointed time for you to enter into your promise and He will honor his schedule. So Rest Well knowing that you never have to question God's presence or take matters into your own hands because you are trusting and believing in God's amazing promises.

"Yes. I'll stay with you, I'll protect you wherever you go, and I'll bring you back to this very ground. I'll stick with you until I've done everything I promised you" (Genesis 28:15, The Message).

Dear God

I will no longer question Your presence because You love me, You watch over me and will bring me into all that You have promised.

Notes

REST WELL KNOWING THAT GOD'S PROMISES ARE NOT UP FOR NEGOTIATION.

Sometimes you have a set-back and you are not where you want to be in your forward progress. You had goals and deadlines that have not been met and the company you keep means well when they tell you to settle for less and to go with your "plan B." You have allowed your negative thoughts to form a partnership with your emotions and the outcome is not good. Your prayer life has become more like a hostage negotiation where you are bargaining with the voice of doubt. But now you know better and realize that God does not need to honor your deadline to fulfill His word. You know that your "plan B" is to remain fully prepared for your harvest of blessings because you're not giving up. So Rest Well knowing that from heaven's perspective, God's promises are still Yes and Amen and that is not even up for discussion.

"Not one of all the Lord's good promises to the house of Israel failed; every one was fulfilled" (Joshua 21:45, NIV).

Dear God

I will not exchange my birthright because of fear or doubt and instead I will remain steadfast on the full measure of what You have promised.

Notes

REST WELL KNOWING THAT FROM HEAVEN'S PERSPECTIVE YOU ARE ELIGIBLE FOR AN UPGRADE.

Sometimes you live so far beneath your promise simply because you don't know your true identity. You are still wearing an outdated label by living in the shadows of your mistake. Elevating your expectations and believing for better seems like a great idea, but the voice of doubt causes you to question not only your worthiness, but also your audacity to think God would shine His face upon you and your mess. But now you know better and realize that the labels: Forgiven, Redeemed, and New Creation are the only labels that truly matter. You know that the reason you have the audacity to believe God is because your mess-up has been drowned in God's Sea of Forgiveness and your come-up is already written into your story. So Rest Well knowing that in spite of what your situation looks like, from heaven's perspective you are eligible for a divine upgrade of abundant blessings.

"The thief comes only in order to steal and kill and destroy. I came that they may have and enjoy life, and have it in abundance (to the full, till it overflows)" (John 10:10, Amplified).

Dear God

I embrace my divine upgrade with confidence knowing that my worthiness is not based on what I've done, but on who You are.

Notes

Preparation Process

REST WELL KNOWING THAT THE WILDERNESS IS NOT TO PUNISH YOU, IT IS TO DISCONNECT YOU FROM WHAT YOU LEFT, AND PREPARE YOU FOR WHAT HAS BEEN PROMISED.

Sometimes it is so hard to keep a positive attitude in the middle of a wilderness experience. You thought being in bondage was bad, but the wilderness seems worse. It's tempting to think that God must be punishing you for some secret sin from your past. The company you keep treats you just like Job's friends and speaks condemnation while attempting to convince you that God is trying to teach you a lesson. But now you know better and realize that God is not mean or spiteful; He doesn't keep a record of your wrongs or hold anything against you because He only sees you as His beloved child who is forgiven. You know that Calvary eliminated condemnation in spite of what your friends may think. So Rest Well knowing that the wilderness is a very temporary situation that is disconnecting you from what you left and it is preparing you for what has been promised.

"Jesus replied, 'You don't understand now what I'm doing, but it will be clear enough to you later'" (John 13:7, The Message).

Dear God

I may not understand this temporary season but I trust You and I'm confident that it's preparing me for my promise.

Notes

REST WELL KNOWING THAT THE LENGTH OF YOUR PROCESS IS JUST AN INDICATION OF THE MAGNITUDE OF YOUR BLESSING.

Sometimes it gets so frustrating trying to remain confident in your promise when you are still going through your process. It seems like you have been preparing long enough. It is time to either "microwave" your harvest or you may end up going hungry, never experiencing the desires of your heart. As much as you want to experience God's best, this "preparation thing" is a bit too much. But now you know better and realize that God is setting you up for success. He does not give you anything half-baked or second-rate. Just like the largest planes need the longest runways because they are flying higher and going farther, your process is going to give new meaning to soaring on wings like eagles. So Rest Well knowing that the length of your process and the expansiveness of your process is just an indication of the magnitude of your blessings.

"No one's ever seen or heard anything like this, never so much as imagined anything quite like it, what God has arranged for those who love Him" (1 Corinthians 2:9, The Message).

Dear God

I refuse to grow weary during my time of preparation because I know it's just an indication of the magnitude of my blessing.

Notes

REST WELL KNOWING THAT GOD IS PREPARING YOU FOR WHERE YOU ARE GOING, NOT FOR WHAT YOU LEFT.

Sometimes the hardest part of making a destiny decision is embracing your new identity. You know there is major purpose for your life and greatness inside of you. The challenge is trying to still fit into the old things while being shaped for the new things that God is doing in your life. You don't want to rock the boat or disrupt the expectations of others. But now you know better and realize that you do not need to fit into an old situation, God created you to stand out and shine your light. You have to depart from some things before you can arrive at your promise, and God is not concerned by your rocking the boat. He turned over tables to see purpose prevail. So Rest Well knowing God is preparing you for the awesome place that you are going, not for what you left.

"For we are God's workmanship, created in Christ Jesus to do good works, which God prepared in advance for us to do" (Ephesians 2:10, NIV).

Dear God

I commit to preparing for my purpose, to embracing Your will even if I have to rock the boat because I want my light to shine for your glory.

Notes

REST WELL KNOWING THAT GOD HAS NOT FORGOTTEN YOU, HE IS PREPARING YOU.

Sometimes you can press into your promise for so long, that it's easy to start wondering if somehow God has forgotten about you. The voice of doubt tells you that it doesn't make sense for people you consider less-qualified for God's blessings to experience the desires of their heart. But now you know better and realize that what God has planned requires you to stay in your lane and not count someone else's blessings, because it causes you to lose sight of your own. You know that on the other side of victory, you will realize that you were being made ready for greatness beyond what you could ask or think, and He forgets your sins because your name is written in the palm of His hand. So Rest Well knowing that God has not forgotten you, He is simply preparing you and fulfilling His promise to you.

"Be still in the presence of the Lord, and wait patiently for Him to act. Don't worry about evil people who prosper or fret about their wicked schemes" (Psalm 37:7, NLT).

Dear God

I run my race in my lane grateful for my current blessings, I embrace my process and anticipate my promises.

Notes

REST WELL KNOWING THAT PRUNING IS NOT A PUNISHMENT, IT IS THE PROCESS FOR ABUNDANCE.

Sometimes your emotions spiral out of control when something gets cut out of your life. Negative thoughts cause you to wonder how much God loves you if He was willing to cut that person or situation out of your life. You think that perhaps happy endings are just not your portion. The company you keep tries to encourage you by saying it was for the best, but you are not trying to hear their comments because it feels like the worst. But now you know better and realize that what got cut was a fruitless situation that did not ressemble God's best. You know that when you step away from your feelings and get into faith, it is obvious God is working for your good. Whatever got cut was just the first step in preparing for your promise. So Rest Well knowing that a divine pruning is simply the set-up for a greater blessing.

"He cuts off every branch of mine that doesn't produce fruit, and He prunes the branches that do bear fruit so they will produce even more" (John 15:2, NLT).

Dear God

I will not despise my pruning process because I know that ultimately You plan for me to live an abundant and fruitful life.

Notes

REST WELL KNOWING THAT THE SPECTATORS WHO WATCHED YOU GO THROUGH, ARE NOW GOING TO BEAR WITNESS THAT YOU CAME OUT.

Sometimes what makes your process so difficult is the self-imposed shame you have embraced. It's so hard to face your circle of influence knowing they have seen your struggle, seen your mistake. It causes you to become resentful of your restoration process simply because you feel like a public spectacle, like your mess-up is on full display, and the gossipers are having a field day at your expense. But now you know better and realize there is no shame in what you have been through because you are an overcomer who brings glory to your God. You know that the reason people are watching is because God is setting your table so every gossiper and naysayer can see divine restoration at work. So Rest Well knowing that spectators are going to give an eye witness account of how God prepared you, He restored you, and He blessed you.

"You prepare a feast for me in the presence of my enemies. You honor me by anointing my head with oil. My cup overflows with blessings" (Psalm 23:5, NLT).

Dear God

I exchange my shame for Your beauty, for Your garment of praise knowing that You are preparing me for blessings beyond my dreams.

Notes

REST WELL KNOWING THAT PREPARATION TIME IS NEVER A WASTE OF TIME, IT IS AN INVESTMENT OF TIME THAT PAYS GREAT REWARDS.

Sometimes you get frustrated by your process and lose sight of your promise. All you can think about is how much time you spent on the backside of the mountain not doing anything meaningful. The voice of doubt tells you that surely you must have missed your moment, that you have been getting ready for so long and now it is as if you are all dressed up with nowhere to go. But now you know better and realize that God is so strategic that He will prepare you on the backside of the mountain with something that seems mundane, but it has equipped you to become a giant-slayer. You know that He does not need to rush the process because He redeems the time. So Rest Well knowing that you have not wasted any time, God moves suddenly and your process has made sure that you are prepared for divine accomplishments and mind-blowing experiences.

"And now, O Lord God, you are God and your words are true, and you have promised this good thing to your servant" (2 Samuel 7:28, New King James Version).

Dear God

I trust Your process because I know You give great rewards and I am a giant-slayer in the making.

Notes

REST WELL KNOWING THAT THE BEST IS YET TO COME BECAUSE GOD ALWAYS FINISHES WHAT HE STARTS.

Sometimes your joy and your peace are compromised because you are not living the way you thought. Life feels lonely, empty and incomplete, and the voice of doubt plays on your insecurities by telling you that what you're believing is way beyond what you deserve. It seems like God left you hanging somewhere between who you were and who He said you would be. But now you know better and realize that the power that raised Christ from the dead is the same power that will turn your situation around. You know that you aren't hanging out on a limb, you are standing with confidence on your promise, and God said you are complete and lacking nothing. So Rest Well knowing that in spite of whatever happened to you, God did not give up on you because He knew the end from the beginning and He always finishes everything He started.

"There has never been the slightest doubt in my mind that the God who started this great work in you would keep at it and bring it to a flourishing finish on the very day Christ Jesus appears" (Philippians 1:6, The Message).

Dear God

I am fully persuaded that You started a process in me with the end in mind and You have an amazing plan and a great strategy for my victory.

Notes

Trusting God

REST WELL KNOWING THAT WHEN GOD RESTED ON THE SEVENTH DAY, IT WASN'T BECAUSE HE WAS TIRED, IT WAS BECAUSE HE WAS FINISHED.

One of the greatest tricks of the enemy is to convince you that your faith is missing something. Your feelings waste time trying to identify a blind spot in your faith, something more that you need to do, to get God on your side, to move on your behalf or show up in your situation. The voice of doubt wants you to believe that walking in victory is too complicated. But now you know better and realize the word is crystal clear that God gave you all of His power and authority to accomplish your purpose and give Him glory. You know that you do not need to do anything, you just need to trust God with everything because your faith is more than enough. So Rest Well knowing that God did not rest on the seventh day because He was tired, He rested because He was finished and your victory was already won.

"And I am praying that you will put into action the generosity that comes from your faith as you understand and experience all the good things we have in Christ" (Philemon 1:6, NLT).

Dear God

I release my deficits mentality and I am secure in the knowledge that the finished work of Calvary has made my faith complete.

Notes

REST WELL KNOWING THAT YOU DO NOT NEED TO SETTLE FOR BEING A "CRUMB CHRISTIAN" BECAUSE GOD WANTS TO BLESS YOU WITH THE WHOLE LOAF.

Sometimes humility is one of the most misunderstood concepts of faith. You think that settling for less, living beneath your promise, accepting whatever comes your way will somehow make you more humble and ultimately a better Christian. The voice of doubt reinforces this concept by telling you that people who expect better don't know how to be content with what they have. But now you know better and realize that it is God's good pleasure to have you overtaken with blessings that bring Him glory. You know that you are very content where you are, you are convinced that God is going to grant you the desires of your heart, and His blessings make you rich without adding worry. So Rest Well knowing that you are not going to settle for being a crumb-snatching, make-do Christian because God is blessing you with the whole loaf.

"So if you sinful people know how to give good gifts to your children, how much more will your heavenly Father give good gifts to those who ask Him" (Matthew 7:9, NLT).

Dear God

I am content in You and fully convinced of Your goodness, your amazing plan and your awesome promises.

Notes

REST WELL KNOWING THAT YOUR MARCHING LOOKS FOOLISH UNTIL THE WALLS COME DOWN AND YOUR SHOUT GOES UP.

Sometimes what makes obedience so difficult is public opinion. You believe God; however, the moment you step out of your prayer closet and into real life, you are bombarded by doubt and criticism. People think you are crazy for being all-in with your obedience. You are wondering if you really need to act on what God said or if you can trust and believe it from inside your comfort zone. But now you know better and realize that faith without work is dead, that people who live the desires of their heart acted on God's word, and that what has been promised to you is far greater than what other people think about you. So Rest Well knowing that it's okay if you feel a little foolish while you are marching, when the walls come down and your shout goes up, you will look very wise and be considered extremely blessed.

"But if you look carefully into the perfect law that sets you free, and if you do what it says and don't forget what you heard, then God will bless you for doing it" (James 1:25, NLT).

Dear God

I remain obedient to You, to Your word and Your will for my life knowing that the path You have for me leads to my promise.

Notes

Sometimes you get overly-consumed by your situation and your emotions begin to misrepresent God's abilities. Your circumstances are saying it has been too long, there isn't enough, and there's no way out. The voice of doubt reinforces the negativity by reminding you that things don't look good. The company you keep is pronouncing the benediction on your dreams and helping you accept your inevitable defeat. But now you know better and realize that from heaven's perspective, lack, time, and limitations are irrelevant. You know that God is not looking for a way to bring you out, He has already prepared the way. One word from God brings provision in time of need, eyesight to the blind, and the ability to get up out of a sick bed. So Rest Well knowing that your mustard seed faith is more than enough to experience sudden moments of abundant blessings and supernatural victory.

"He does great things too marvelous to understand. He performs countless miracles" (Job 5:9, NLT).

Dear God

I walk by faith, not by sight so in spite of what it looks like, You are a God of abundant blessings and numerous miracles.

Notes

REST WELL KNOWING THAT YOUR RAM IN THE BUSH WAS PREPARED BEFORE YOU TOOK THE FIRST STEP OF FAITH.

Sometimes you want to make a "boss" move, to believe in your promise and expect the desires of your heart. But your situation says that it is a struggle, sacrifice, or maybe even impossible. It seems like what God is asking you to do will require too much commitment and sacrifice on your part. Logic says to play it safe, that a bird in the hand is better than two in the bush. But now you know better and realize that God's supernatural provision defies all manner of logic. You know that your commitment to Him will always bless you far more than it cost you. You can release what is in your hand because you trust in His more-than-capable hands. So Rest Well knowing that you never have to question anything you give up for God, He provided your ram in the bush before you even took your first step of faith.

"If God didn't hesitate to put everything on the line for us, embracing our condition and exposing Himself to the worst by sending His own Son, is there anything else He wouldn't gladly and freely do for us?" (Romans 8:32, The Message).

Dear God

I appreciate that my steps are ordered and that when I surrender something to You it comes back to me with excellence and increase.

Notes

REST WELL KNOWING THAT THE SAME GOD WHO SENT PROVISION INTO THE WILDERNESS IS SENDING YOU A SOLUTION FOR YOUR SITUATION.

Sometimes in the midst of your circumstance, trusting God does not seem like a good idea. Your eye is off the prize because you are distracted by all the chaos and lack that have created a customized wilderness experience. Turning back seems to be the only logical option because the eyes of your understanding are blind. All you can see is what's working against you and it is tempting to be disappointed by the people who are not helping you. But now you know better and realize that as a believer, God is for you, and therefore who could dare be against you? You know that you are not relying on people because you are trusting in God and your renewed mind allows you to see the hand of God. So Rest Well knowing that the same faithful God who sent provision into the wilderness is sending you a divine solution to turn your situation around.

"The Friend, the Holy Spirit whom the Father will send at my request, will make everything plain to you. He will remind you of all the things I have told you" (John 14:26, The Message).

Dear God

I thank You for the gift of the Holy Spirit that is teaching me what I need to know and I speak by faith that my situation is turning around.

Notes

REST WELL KNOWING THAT YOUR SITUATION MAY SAY TO TURN BACK, BUT GOD IS MORE THAN ABLE TO TURN IT AROUND.

Sometimes you just want to give up on your promised place because of all the "Ites" you keep encountering. You are looking at your opposition through the lens of fear and believe you are a mere grasshopper among giants. Then you start leaning on your own understanding and wonder why God promised you His best, but then made barriers around it, making it so difficult to experience. But now you know better and realize anything coming against you is actually beneath you because God makes footstools out of your enemy. You know that you can trample over anything because angels are holding you up with their hands so you will not even hurt your foot. You have the right report which says you will press forward and occupy. So Rest Well knowing that you don't need to consider going back because God has already orchestrated your turnaround in your favor.

"Stay on the path that the Lord your God has commanded you to follow. Then you will live long and have a prosperous life in the land you are about to enter and occupy" (Deuteronomy 5:33. NLT).

Dear God

I will stay the course knowing the direction of faith is always clear and I trust You to take me into the place You have promised me.

Notes

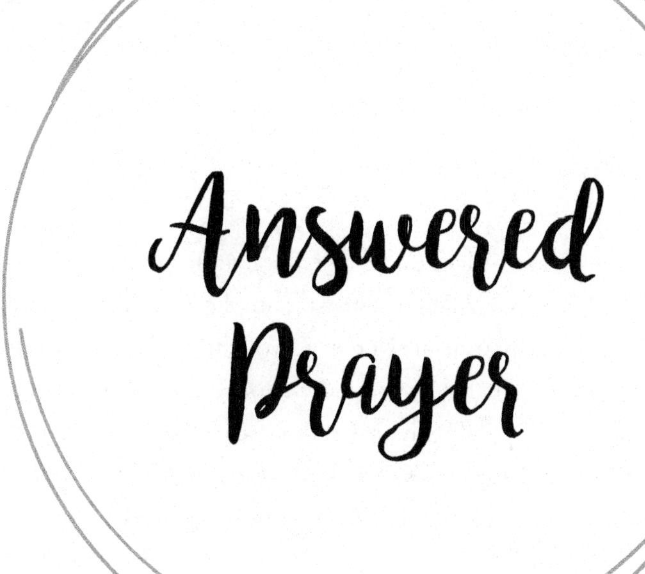
Answered
Prayer

REST WELL KNOWING THAT YOUR MEASURE OF FAITH IS HOW YOU ACCESS THE ANSWER TO YOUR PRAYERS.

One of the greatest tricks of the enemy is confusion, because when you are confused, then your faith seems so complicated. You don't have a clue how to get your prayers answered, so you start taking advice from popular culture and think that if you draw enough attention to yourself, heaven will take notice. Desperation starts to set in because you needed your breakthrough to happen yesterday! But now you know better and realize that although the enemy traffics in confusion, speaking the word of God brings clarity to all things. You know that since God numbers the hair on your head, surely He has notice of you and He said be confident when you pray that He hears you. Desperate times don't call for desperate measures, they call for your measure of faith. So Rest Well knowing that the answer to your prayer comes from your measure of faith.

"And whatever you ask for in prayer, having faith and [really] believing, you will receive" (Matthew 21:22, Amplified Bible).

Dear God

I speak Your word to bring clarity into my situation knowing that my mustard seed measurement of faith will bring forth the answer to my prayers.

Notes

REST WELL KNOWING THAT FROM HEAVEN'S PERSPECTIVE, WHAT YOU PRAYED FOR HAS ALREADY BEEN PREPARED BY GOD.

Sometimes it is so hard to know that God heard your prayers. You have asked in faith and now you are waiting with expectancy on the answer to your problem, the provision for your purpose, the desires of your heart. The problem seems to be that the more you ask, the more God seems to be silent. The voice of doubt decides to take advantage of your inability to hear from God and causes you to wrestle with unbelief. But now you know better and realize that God said to ask according to His will because He hears you. His silence is not an indication of His absence, as He has already spoken to you directly in His word and gives you His authority to experience His abundance. So Rest Well knowing that from heaven's perspective it is finished and God has already prepared the answer to your prayers.

"But when you ask him, be sure that your faith is in God alone. Do not waver, for a person with divided loyalty is as unsettled as a wave of the sea that is blown and tossed by the wind" (James 1:6, NLT).

Dear God

I know You speak in a still, small whisper so I silence all forms of negativity so I can confidently hear from You and stand steadfast in my faith.

Notes

REST WELL KNOWING THAT IN SPITE OF WHAT IT LOOKS LIKE, GOD HEARS EVERY PRAYER AND WIPES EVERY TEAR.

Sometimes it seems like your world has been turned upside-down with senseless acts of ill will. Your hurt causes you to cry out "really God? How much more madness do I have to experience? How much more "wilding out" is my situation going to get? The negativity overwhelms you and causes fear, distrust and even depression. But now you know better and realize that when you open the eyes of your understanding, you will see the hand of God at work in your situation. You may have had a painful experience, but weeping is temporary, joy is your birthright. You do not need to fear anything because whatever is coming against you will bow down at the name of Jesus. So Rest Well knowing that in spite of what it looks like, God hears your prayers, He wipes your tears, and turns your sorrow to joy.

"Before they call out, I'll answer. Before they've finished speaking, I'll have heard" (Isaiah 65:24, The Message).

Dear God

I am so grateful that regardless of what I have experienced when I call out to You, I have no doubt that You hear me, You guide me and You comfort me.

Notes

REST WELL KNOWING THAT ON THE OTHER SIDE OF VICTORY YOU WILL REALIZE THAT WHAT YOU THOUGHT WAS OPPOSITION WAS ACTUALLY A DIVINE OPPORTUNITY TO PROVE GOD AT HIS WORD.

Sometimes faith is just theoretical, a good idea. You are a regular church attendant, you can recite some scripture, and you believe in the power of prayer, but then out of nowhere, trouble shows up at your door. You feel like your faith is failing or that you don't have enough of it because you have never been prepared for anything like this. But now you know better and realize that the faith you have been professing and practicing is for such a time as this. You know that no weapon formed against you shall prosper, what is in you is greater than anything coming against you, and that opposition offers a front row seat to God's faithfulness. So Rest Well knowing that your victory is at-hand and you are going to be so grateful that you had the opportunity to experience firsthand that God honors His word and it never returns void.

"The Lord your God will restore your fortunes. He will have mercy on you and gather you back from all the nations where he has scattered you" (Deuteronomy 30:3, NLT).

Dear God

I know You will use my opposition as an opportunity for me to experience Your divine restoration and abundant grace.

Notes

REST WELL KNOWING THAT YOU CAN PREPARE FOR WHAT YOU'VE PRAYED FOR BECAUSE YOU ACTED ON WHAT YOU BELIEVE.

Sometimes you question your faith move because it really goes against your play-it-safe approach to life. People are questioning your judgment because you have stepped outside of your self-imposed box of limitations and you hear comments such as "you've changed." Eventually you start to wonder if you made the right decision, and whether you should simply return to the comfort of mediocrity. But now you know better and realize that exceeding and abundant blessings come from taking God at His word and then acting on what He said. You know that your faith is too powerful and God's promises are too awesome for you to remain on the sidelines of your own life. You are expectant of your blessings because you know God already prepared your harvest. So Rest Well knowing that you can prepare for what you prayed for because you were bold enough to act on what you believe.

"Now someone may argue, 'Some people have faith; others have good deeds.' But I say, 'How can you show me your faith if you don't have good deeds? I will show you my faith by my good deeds.'" (James 2:18, NLT).

Dear God

I am filled with anticipation because I know You answer my prayers of faith and my acts of obedience with abundant rewards.

Notes

REST WELL KNOWING THAT GOD WILL ANSWER YOUR PRAYERS WITH WHAT YOU NEED, EVEN WHEN YOU DON'T KNOW WHAT TO ASK.

Sometimes you find yourself going to God in such a state of confusion that you don't even know what to pray. Staying where you are is not an option, and you can't take another moment of "more of the same," yet you want to believe God has a better plan than what you're currently experiencing. Your emotions want to cry out to God but don't even know what to say. But now you know better and realize that God is so faithful. He answers the prayers in your heart even when your mind doesn't know what to ask. You know that confusion is a distraction because His word and His plan bring clarity. So Rest Well knowing that in spite of your uncertainty about what comes next, you can be confidently assured that God hears you and He answers you according to His loving kindness and perfect will.

"And He who searches our hearts knows the mind of the Spirit, because the Spirit intercedes for the saints in accordance with God's will" (Romans 8:27, NIV).

Dear God

I am grateful that You love me enough to answer my prayers with what I need even when I'm uncertain of what to ask.

Notes

REST WELL KNOWING THAT HEAVEN HEARS YOUR PRAYERS EVEN IN THE MIDST OF YOUR MESS.

Sometimes in the midst of your mess, you adopt a religious mindset that causes you to avoid God until you get yourself together, or until you feel that you deserve to be loved by God. Your negative thoughts rationalize that if you could just stay quiet and not connect with God, then heaven won't notice your mess-up. You feel judged by others and unworthy of a relationship with God. But now you know better and realize that God has extended His grace and mercy to you for such a time as this; an opportunity to run your race in the right lane. He honors the prayers of the righteous which is not based on your behavior, it is because He is your Savior. So Rest Well knowing that God does not ignore you in your mess, He extends His love, He hears your prayers and offers His grace to clean it up.

"The Lord directs the steps of the godly. He delights in every detail of their lives. Though they stumble, they will never fall, for the Lord holds them by the hand" (Psalm 37:23-24, New Living Translation).

Dear God

I receive your perfect love with a grateful heart and I embrace Your grace by shifting my focus from my mess-up to looking up to you, the source of my help and strength.

Notes

A Note from Stacey

It's amazing how much can change in 90 days! If 21 days of doing something forms a habit, then 90 days of studying and reflecting on what God has said, can change your life! I encourage you to refer back to this Devotional often to celebrate your progress, to remind yourself of all of God's amazing promises, and to let go of anything that isn't serving you well, anything that entertains unbelief and plants seeds of doubt. My hope is that you will truly receive the grace and mercy that goes before you and let God's peace guide you.

I applaud your commitment to the journey and it is my sincere prayer that as you go through this journal, you will be encouraged in your spirit, strengthened in your faith and have the ability to Rest Well.

Blessings,

Stacey

Printed in Great Britain
by Amazon